Diet recommendations for Short Bowel Syndrome

Please check these recommendations always with a nutrition consultant, therapist, doctor or dietician. The recipes and the list of ingredients are supporting the conventional medical therapy.
The calorie disclosures of fresh ingredients (fruit and vegetables) vary according to quality and time of harvest. The contents were checked by a dietician and a nutrition consultant for the Traditional Chinese Medicine (TCM).

Author:
©2017 Josef Miligui
www.ebns.at

AF200099

Source:
The lists are created from the EBNS database for nutritional counseling. The database is used by dietitians, therapists and doctors for advising the patient / client.

Literature:
The specialist literature and the training documents of the German and Austrian dietary and traditional Chinese medicine serve as a knowledge base. We have used the documents as a basis of knowledge, adapted it to our experience and completed them.
http://di-book.com

Title Photo:
©2008 Erika Weixlbaumer

Production and publishing:
BoD – Books on Demand, Norderstedt
ISBN 9783746043012

Diet recommendations for DIETETICS - Gastrointestinal tract - Small intestine and large intestine - Short Bowel Syndrome

1   Treatment strategy

Regenerate the intestinal mucosa, eat easily digestible food.
Eat slowly and chew the food well to prevents stoma blockages and flatulence.
Ensure sufficient liquid of at least 2 liters daily - but not with meals, so that sufficient absorption of the food
 can take place. Pay attention to their temperature. Too cold or too hot drinks can speed up the emptying
rhythm.
The fruit acid of concentrated fruit juices and vinegar, but also spicy spices can irritate the skin in the
environment of the stoma.
Fiber-rich foods can clog the stoma exit (beef, asparagus, cabbage, cabbage).

2   Avoid

Acidic, whitening, fiber-rich foods.

3 Breakfast

kkal. per serving

Apple - banana cream	110
Apricot and cranberry ice cream	106
Banana Soymilk	125
Barley and vegetable soup	281
Barley mash with berries	112
Barley mash with plums	106
Barley soup	265
Carrot and rice gruel soup	101
Compote from apples	67
Compote of local fruit and dried fruit	45
Corn coffee with cardamom	3
Couscous Salad	338
Cranberry juice	43
Grated apple	120
Grated carrots with apple	74
Hearty polenta mash	262
Miso soup with tofu	51
Noodles with Vegetable and tomato sauce	561
Oat Congee	162
Oatmeal soup with spring onion and carrots	134
Polenta with peach	197
Potato with dandelion salad	162
Puréed banana	144
Rice congee with carrots and fennel	131
Rice with parsnips	206
Roasted barley patties	398
Roasted millet with plum compote	139
Rosemary Potatoes	188
Supplementary nutrition	1045
Tea Black tea (Russian tea)	7
Tea from anise	2
Tender fennel vegetables - also for babies from 6th month	70
Vegetable bowl with tofu and curry on rice	162
Vegetable miso soup with tofu	106

4 Snack

Apple - banana cream	110
Barley mash with berries	112
Grated carrots with apple	74
Month porridge - also for babies from 7th month	157

5 Lunch

6 Afternoon

7 Dinner

8   Any time

9   Recipes

(recommendable) = You can use more.
(little) = You should use less than specified or omit.

9.1   Antipasti

Improves blood circulation, anti-inflammatory, relieves pain. Diuretic, promotes digestion, reduces blood pressure. antioxidativ, antibacterial, affects anorexia, improves digestion, flatulence, stomach weakness, Cooking time approx. 40 min
Calories p. portion: 100
3 portions
Allergens:

Quantity of ingredients:
Coriander 1/2 teaspoon / 2g. (yes)
Tomato 4 pieces / 200g. (yes)
Salt 1 pinch / 0,5g. (little)
Aubergine 1 piece / 300g. (yes)
Olive oil 1 table spoon / 15g. (little)
Lemon peel 1/2 piece / 3g. (little)
Pepperoni 1 piece / 5g. (little)
Basil (fresh) 8 leaves / 5g. (yes)
Zucchini 5/8 oz / 200g. (recommended)
Lemon juice 1 table spoon / 10g. (little)

Cooking instructions:
Preheat the oven to 250 degrees Celsius and bake the hot peppers until the bowl becomes dark (about 20 minutes). Cover the hot peppers with a clear film and allow to cool. Peel the skin and cut into strips about 2 cm wide. Cut tomatoes in half and spread with oil in slices of aubergine and bake in the oven at 200 degrees golden brown (about 10 minutes) Fry the zucchini slices in the grill pan (without fat).
Mix everything together, mix the marinade of olive oil, salt and lemon peel and pour over the vegetables, sprinkle with coriander. Leave for 1 hour.

9.2 Apple - banana cream

Regulates gastrointestinal function, provides vitamin C, cholesterol lowering, reduces inflammation, diuretic, improves blood circulation.
Cooking time approx. 15 min
Calories p. portion: 110
4 portions
Allergens:

Quantity of ingredients:
Apple (sour) 7/8 lbs / 400g. (little)
Lemon peel 1/2 piece / 2g. (little)
Sugar brown 2 teaspoons / 6g. (little)
Cinnamon sticks 1 piece / 0g. (yes)
Banana 1 piece / 150g. (recommended)
Orange juice 1/2 piece / 50g. (little)
Lemon juice 1 table spoon / 10g. (little)
Water 3/4 cup - 6 oz / 200g. (yes)
Orange peel 1/4 piece / 5g. (little)
Acerola fruit nectar or powder 1 teaspoon / 2g. (little)

Cooking instructions:
Cut the apple into fine slices, bring water to boil and add the apple slices, orange- and lemon peel, sugar and cinnamon and simmer about 7 minutes. The apples should be almost soft. Remove acerola and the cinnamon stick.
Mix the apple, the banana, the orange juice and the lemon juice.

9.3 Apricot and cranberry ice cream

Forces resistance to infections, good to fight oral mucosal inflammation, diarrhea. Has a positive effect on the urinary tract.
Cooking time approx. 5 min
Calories p. portion: 106
2 portions
Allergens:

Quantity of ingredients:
Water 1/4 cup / 50g. (yes)
Cranberry 2 table spoons / 45g. (yes)
Apricots 3/4 lbs / 350g. (little)

Cooking instructions:
Mix the apricot juice with the cranberry syrup. Fill the juice into little molds, place in the freezer and let it freeze in about 3 hours.

9.4 Banana Soymilk

Good to fight loss of appetite, oral mucosa inflammation. Strengthens body energy, promotes stomach-spleen harmony, promotes digestion, regulates gastrointestinal function. Relieves pain, detoxifying, bactericide.
Cooking time approx. 5 min
Calories p. portion: 126
2 portions
Allergens: E

Quantity of ingredients:
Cinnamon ground 1 pinch / 1g. (yes)
Banana 1 piece / 120g. (recommended)
Honey 1 teaspoon / 3g. (little)
Acerola fruit nectar or powder 1 teaspoon / 2g. (little)
Soybean milk 1 1/2 cups / 400g. (yes)

Cooking instructions:
Cut the banana into pieces, puree them with soy milk, acerola, honey and cinnamon with the mixing stick.

9.5 Barley and vegetable soup

Supports urination, detoxifying, promotes spleen and liver, reduces blood pressure, strengthens immune system, prevents cancer, reduces radiation damage, promotes digestion, helps to digest fat, harmonizes.
Cooking time approx. 2 hours
Calories p. portion: 281
3 portions
Allergens: AGL

Quantity of ingredients:
Barley 1 cup / 120g. (yes)
Pepper (ground) 1 pinch / 0,5g. (little)
Parsley 1 teaspoon / 3g. (yes)
Shiitake, dried 1/8 oz / 4g. (little)
Celery sticks 2 branches / 20g. (yes)

Tomato 1 piece / 50g. (yes)
Onion (shallot) 1 piece / 20g. (little)
Cumin (Caraway seed) 1 knife tip / 0,5g. (yes)
Sunflower oil 1 table spoon / 10g. (little)
French beans Handful / 30g. (little)
Peas, green 5/8 lbs - 8oz / 250g. (little)
Carrot 2 pieces / 150g. (recommended)
Water 1 cup / 250g. (yes)
Butter Bio 1 teaspoon / 3g. (little)
Salt 1 pinch / 1g. (little)

Cooking instructions:
Soak the barley in the evening for the next day. Soak the mushrooms separately at the next day. Brown onion and cumin in oil, then boil with water. Add the chopped vegetables, some salt, the barley and the shiitake mushrooms and cook everything to a thick soup. At the end, season with pepper, parsley and a little butter.

9.6 Barley mash with berries

Diuretic, forcing spleen, supports urination, laxative, strengthens kidney, promotes digestion, detoxifying, promotes perspiration, reduces blood lipids, stimulates, dissolves stagnation.
Cooking time approx. 2 hours
Calories p. portion: 113
5 portions
Allergens: A

Quantity of ingredients:
Lemon Balm (fresh) 2-4 leaves / 3g. (yes)
Water 10 cups / 1200g. (yes)
Barley 1 cup / 120g. (yes)
Raspberry 5/8 lbs - 8oz / 250g. (yes)
Cocoa 1 pinch / 1g. (little)
Barley malt 1 table spoon / 15g. (yes)
Ginger fresh 2 slices / 2g. (yes)
Cardamom 3 capsules / 1g. (recommended)
Salt 1 pinch / 1g. (little)

Cooking instructions:
Boil the barley with water, ginger and cardamom pods in a large saucepan. Close pot with a lid and cook over low heat for about 2 hours.

For 2 servings of cooked barley porridge, place about 2 ladles in a bowl. Stir with sunflower seeds, malt, cocoa powder and a pinch of salt. Stir fresh berries into the porridge and serve sprinkled with fresh mint or lemon balm.

Tip: The pre-cooked barley porridge (without fruit) can be stored well in the refrigerator and used for sweet or savory dishes, e.g. with stewed vegetables or fruit seasoned compote.

9.7 Barley mash with plums

Promotes spleen, diuretic, forcing spleen, supports urination, relaxes, reduces internal heat.
Cooking time approx. 25 min
Calories p. portion: 107
5 portions
Allergens: AG

Quantity of ingredients:
Sugar cane sugar 1/2 teaspoon / 2g. (little)
Plum 1 cup / 120g. (little)
Butter Bio 2 teaspoons / 6g. (little)
Barley 1 cup / 120g. (yes)
Water 10 cups / 1200g. (yes)

Cooking instructions:
Grind coarse the barley and roast it dry. Add hot water, add ginger and cardamom and let it swell to a pulp in low heat. Core the plums and boil for 10 minutes with a little water. At the end, add the stewed plums, a little butter and sweetener.

Variant: If you want to go fast, you can use barley flakes instead of shot.

9.8 Barley soup

Diuretic, forcing spleen, supports urination, stimulates liver function, antioxidativ, promotes digestion, detoxifying, reduces blood lipids, stimulates, dissolves stagnation.

Cooking time approx. 25 min
Calories p. portion: 265
2 portions
Allergens: A

Quantity of ingredients:
Salt 1 pinch / 1g. (little)
Ginger fresh 1/2 teaspoon / 1g. (yes)
Barley 1 cup / 120g. (yes)
Parsley 2 table spoons / 30g. (yes)
Olive oil 1 table spoon / 10g. (little)
Water 1 1/2 cups / 240g. (yes)

Cooking instructions:
Roast the barley in the pan, then grind it to the ground, and boil with
water, some salt and ginger to a mash. Before serving add oil and
parsley.
Variant: You can add a better taste to the dish if you cook it with
prepared vegetable or meat broth.

9.9   Basic recipe for a beef broth (clear)

Strengthens muscles, tendons and bones, reduces blood pressure,
strengthens immune system, prevents cancer, reduces radiation
damage, stimulates digestion, reduces pain, promotes digestion,
diuretic. Rosemary stimulates digestion.
Cooking time approx. 4-8 hours
Calories p. portion: 114
10 portions
Allergens: O

Quantity of ingredients:
Beef soup meat 1,1 lbs / 500g. (yes)
Parsnip 2 pieces / 300g. (yes)
Vinegar (Red wine vinegar) 1 dash / 3g. (little)
Juniper berry 8 pieces / 6g. (yes)
Salt 1 teaspoon / 5g. (little)
Beef meatbones 5/8 oz / 200g. (little)
Water 3,3 lbs / 1300g. (yes)
Rosemary 1 pinch / 1g. (yes)
Carrot 3 pieces / 210g. (recommended)
Leek 1 piece / 200g. (little)
Lovage 1 stem / 15g. (yes)

Ginger fresh 1/2 teaspoon / 5g. (yes)
Anise (Common Fennel) 2 pieces / 1g. (yes)
Clove 2 pieces / 2g. (yes)
Pimento 6 pieces / 12g. (yes)

Cooking instructions:
Heat water, a dash of red wine vinegar, some juniper berries, a little rosemary, bones and meat till it boils; add carrot, parsnip, leek, ginger, lovage, clove, allspice, star anise and a little salt; simmer for 4-8 hours then strain.
Refrigerate for later use.

9.10 Basic recipe for a chicken broth worming

Strengthens blood, strengthens bone marrow, reduces blood pressure, strengthens immune system, prevents cancer, reduces radiation damage, promotes sweating, dissolves stagnation, good to fight loss of appetite.
Cooking time approx. 2-3 hours
Calories p. portion: 90
9 portions
Allergens: L

Quantity of ingredients:
Ginger fresh 2 slices / 2g. (yes)
Juniper berry 1 teaspoon / 3g. (yes)
Water 4 cup / 900g. (yes)
Bay leaf 3 pieces / 2g. (yes)
Leek 1 stick / 45g. (little)
Fenugreek (Trigonella foenum-graecum) 1 teaspoon / 2g. (yes)
Celery root 1 piece / 500g. (yes)
Carrot 2 pieces / 150g. (recommended)
Chicken meat 1/2 piece / 600g. (little)

Cooking instructions:
Remove chicken parts from fat. Place chicken pieces in a saucepan with hot water and heat till it boils briefly, skimming any resulting foam. Add coarsely chopped vegetables and all spices and cook over medium heat for 2 to 3 hours. Strain the finished soup. Throw away vegetables and bones.
Tip: If you want to use the meat as a soup insert, take out after 45 minutes and return only the bones in the soup.
Refrigerate for later use.

9.11 Basic recipe for a reissue soup (Congee)

Low fat content, for the drainage of the body overweight and high blood pressure.
Cooking time approx. 2-4 hours
Calories p. portion: 140
3 portions
Allergens:

Quantity of ingredients:
Water 6 cups / 700g. (yes)
Rice variety any 1 cup / 120g. (yes)

Cooking instructions:
Cook rice and water in a ratio of about 1: 6. The amount of water determines the thickness of the mash (matter of taste).
Put the rice in a saucepan with a heavy lid. It is important to simmer the rice after a short boil on the slightest flame, otherwise it burns.
Boil the rice for 2-4 hours. The longer he cooks, the more he strengthens.
If you want to eat the dish for breakfast, you can put the rice on just before bedtime.
To be on the safe side, you should first check the behavior of your pot and cooker under observation for a similar amount of time, so that nothing burns.
Refrigerate for later use.

9.12 Basic recipe for a vegetable soup, nutritious

Reduces blood pressure, strengthens immune system, prevents cancer, forcing spleen, dissolves stagnation, promotes weight loss. Good to fight immunodeficiency, high blood pressure, depressions, diabetes, diarrhea, reduces blood lipids.
Cooking time approx. 2-3 hours
Calories p. portion: 48
5 portions
Allergens: L

Quantity of ingredients:
Ginger fresh 1/2 teaspoon / 2g. (yes)
Onion white 1 piece / 60g. (little)
Salt 1 pinch / 1g. (little)
Bay leaf 2 leaves / 1g. (yes)
Lemon 1/2 piece / 25g. (little)

Lovage 1 table spoon / 3g. (yes)
Thyme dried 1 pinch / 1g. (yes)
Carrot 3 pieces / 200g. (recommended)
Water 3 cups / 650g. (yes)
Juniper berry 6 pieces / 6g. (yes)
Parsnip 3/8 lbs - 6oz / 150g. (yes)
Celery root 1 cup / 100g. (yes)
Olive oil 1 table spoon / 4g. (little)

Cooking instructions:
Cut the vegetables into cubes.
Heat oil in hot pot, fry shortly onions and vegetables.
Add cold water, then add ginger, bay leaf and lemon juice.
Season with juniper, thyme and lovage. Cover for 2 - 3 hours on a low heat and simmer.
The used vegetables should be thrown away.
The basic recipe serves as a soup base and to refine vegetables, legumes or cereals.
If you want to eat vegetable soup immediately, add the desired vegetables half an hour before.
Refrigerate for later use.

9.13 Basmati rice + Zucchini tofu dish

Diuretic, supports urination, harmonizes spleen and stomach, reduces flatulence, good to fight body overweight and high blood pressure.
Antioxidativ, promotes digestion, perspiration, reduces blood lipids, forcing spleen.
Cooking time approx. 20 min
Calories p. portion: 146
4 portions
Allergens: E

Quantity of ingredients:
Ginger fresh 1/2 teaspoon / 4g. (yes)
Zucchini 1 piece / 700g. (recommended)
Water 3 cups / 200g. (yes)
Rice Basmati 1/2 cup / 60g. (little)
Coriander 1/2 teaspoon / 4g. (yes)
Soy Tofu 5/8 lbs - 8oz / 250g. (yes)
Olive oil 2 table spoons / 6g. (little)

Cooking instructions:
Cut tofu cubes and marinate with olive oil, tamari, crushed coriander and ginger. Leave at least 1 hour.

Cook Basmati rice with the water. You can season with onion and cardamom.
Roast zucchini and tofu in pan in the hot oil for approx. 5-7 min.
Serve rice and tofu on a plate.
Add the parsley.

Can also be used as a salad for the home and on the go.

9.14 Beef broth

Warming and nourishing, forces.
Cooking time approx. 2-6 hours
Calories p. portion: 125
7 portions
Allergens: L

Quantity of ingredients:
Lemon 2 dashes / 2g. (little)
Ginger fresh 1 inch / 2g. (yes)
Water 4 cup / 1000g. (yes)
Parsley 1 stem / 10g. (yes)
Beef meat 1,1 lbs / 500g. (yes)
Onion white 1 piece / 50g. (little)
Turmeric (yellow root) 1 pinch / 1g. (recommended)
Parsley root 1 piece / 150g. (yes)
Celery root 1 inch / 25g. (yes)
Wakame 1 inch / 1g. (yes)
Coriander 1/2 teaspoon / 2g. (yes)
Bay leaf 2-3 leaves / 2g. (yes)
Beef meatbones 2 pieces / 0g. (little)
Carrot 2 pieces / 100g. (recommended)

Cooking instructions:
In a saucepan with water (enough to cover the meat), add a few drops of lemon juice, a little turmeric, beef and bones, heat till it boils and simmer for a while; then pour away the whole broth, clean the pot, rinse off meat and bones with hot water (this will save you from foaming) and put it back to the saucepan with hot water (amount as you like); add a good pinch of turmeric, carrot, celery, parsley root to the pot; add onion,

bay leaves, coriander, a piece of sliced ginger, a strip of wakame, a stalk of parsley; boil everything together and simmer for 2-6 hours (if the meat is to be used otherwise, take it out of the broth after 1 1/2 - 2 hours, as soon as it is cooked, the bones are returned to the broth); When the cooking time is over, pour the broth through a sieve and discard all ingredients.

Notes: The longer the broth has cooked, the warmer but more nourishing it is. It is after cooling for 3-4 days in the refrigerator durable. The broth can be drunk hot or used as a base for soups with cereals, potatoes and fresh vegetables.

9.15 Beef pumpkin and vegetable stew

Reduces inflammation, improves digestion, reduces blood glucose, strengthens the muscles, tendons and bones, promotes digestion, helps to digest fat.
Cooking time approx. 1 hour
Calories p. portion: 369
4 portions
Allergens: AL

Quantity of ingredients:
Basic recipe for a vegetable soup (nutritious) 1/4 lbs - 4oz / 125g. (yes)
Salt 1 pinch / 1g. (little)
Parsley 1/2 bunch / 30g. (yes)
Peppers powder 1 teaspoon / 2g. (little)
Sugar cane sugar 1 pinch / 1g. (little)
Ground caraway 1 pinch / 1g. (yes)
Pepper (ground) 1 pinch / 0,5g. (little)
Olive oil 2 table spoons / 25g. (little)
Tomato 3/8 lbs - 6oz / 150g. (yes)
Potato 3/4 lbs / 350g. (recommended)
Pumpkin 3/4 lbs / 350g. (yes)
Beef meat 3/4 lbs / 350g. (yes)
White bread (wheat bread) 4 slices / 80g. (yes)
Leek 3/8 lbs - 6oz / 150g. (little)

Cooking instructions:
Dice beef. Peel pumpkin and dice. Cut the leek into rings and dice the peeled potatoes.
Brew the tomatoes with boiling water, peel off the skin and dice.
Steam the meat in olive oil and fill with vegetable stock. Add the

cleaned vegetables. Season with salt, pepper, paprika, cumin and fructose.
Stew for 30 minutes over low heat.
Season again and sprinkle with parsley and serve with white bread.

9.16 Beef salad

Strengths spleen and stomach, strengthens blood, strengthens the muscles, tendons and bones, diuretic, detoxifying, suppresses conversion of sugar into fat, lowers cholesterol, dissolves stagnation.
Cooking time approx. 10 min
Calories p. portion: 249
1 portions
Allergens: O

Quantity of ingredients:
Vinegar (Apple vinegar) 2 teaspoons / 5g. (little)
Onion white 1/2 oz / 20g. (little)
Salt 1 pinch / 0,5g. (little)
Beef meat 1/8 lbs - 2oz / 50g. (yes)
Peppers 1 oz / 30g. (little)
Cucumber (spicy cucumber) 1 oz / 30g. (yes)
Rapeseed oil 2 teaspoons / 5g. (yes)
Pepper (ground) 1 pinch / 0,1g. (little)
Chives 1 table spoon / 7g. (little)
Bread with carob kernel flour 2 slices / 50g. (yes)

Cooking instructions:
Cook the meat with the basic recipe of a beef broth and let it cool down.
Cut into 1 cm slices. Cut the onions into rings, pepper and gherkin into small cubes. Mix all ingredients.
Make the salad marinade with vinegar, oil and salt and pour over, season to taste and strain.

9.17 Beef soup with carrots, leeks, bay leaves

Strengths spleen and stomach, strengthens blood, strengthens the muscles, tendons and bones. Reduces blood pressure, strengthens immune system. Promotes sweating, dissolves stagnation, forcing spleen and stomach, lets urine and bile juice flow.
Cooking time approx. 2-3 hours
Calories p. portion: 194
5 portions
Allergens:

Quantity of ingredients:
Beef meat 1 lbs / 500g. (yes)
Water 2 cup / 450g. (yes)
Bay leaf 3 leaves / 1g. (yes)
Leek 1/2 piece / 150g. (little)
Carrot 2 pieces / 200g. (recommended)
Salt 1 pinch / 0,5g. (little)
Corn Grease (Polenta) 1 table spoon / 10g. (yes)

Cooking instructions:
In a saucepan with water (enough to cover the meat), add beef soup meat or leg slice and simmer for a moment; then pour off the broth, rinse the meat with hot water (this will save you from foaming), clean the pot and put the meat in hot water again; add chopped carrot, leek, corn and bay leaf; simmer until the meat is cooked.

9.18 Carrot and rice gruel soup

Stops diarrhea, good to fight fever, strengthens immune system, reduces blood pressure.
Cooking time approx. 10 min
Calories p. portion: 101
1 portions
Allergens:

Quantity of ingredients:
Salt 1 teaspoon / 4g. (little)
Basic recipe for a rice soup (Congee) 1 cup / 120g. (yes)
Carrot 2 pieces / 100g. (recommended)

Cooking instructions:
Peel and grate carrots. Heat the rice soup (according to the basic recipe) till it boils and add the grated carrots and salt. Cook for 10 minutes.

9.19 Celery and potato cream soup

Reduces blood pressure, strengthens immune system, promotes weight loss. Good to fight immunodeficiency, loss of appetite, flatulence, depressions, diabetes, diarrhea, improves digestion.
Cooking time approx. 45 min
Calories p. portion: 113
4 portions
Allergens: GL

Quantity of ingredients:
Crème fraiche cheese 2 table spoons / 20g. (little)
Onion white 1/2 piece / 25g. (little)
Parsley 1 table spoon / 8g. (yes)
Salt 1 pinch / 1g. (little)
Lemon peel 1/4 piece / 1g. (little)
Ground 1 pinch / 0,5g. (yes)
Nutmeg 1 pinch / 0,5g. (yes)
Basic recipe for a vegetable soup (nutritious) 3 cups / 700g. (yes)
Olive oil 1 table spoon / 10g. (little)
Potato 5/8 oz / 200g. (recommended)

Cooking instructions:
Heat the olive oil in a saucepan lightly. Fry the onions very gently in a mild heat. Pour with vegetable stock according to the basic recipe. Cover and cook for 15 minutes.
Add curd-cut potato, celery, nutmeg, cumin and lemon zest. Spice with salt and cook for 12 minutes. Potatoes and celery should be soft. Remove the lemon peel.
Puree the soup with crème fraiche using a blender. Season the soup with salt.
Arrange the soup in portions with the chopped parsley.

9.20 Chicken soup with egg yolk and parsley

Strengthens blood, strengthens bone marrow, reduces blood pressure, strengthens immune system. Parsley stimulates liver function, harmonizes liver and spleen, strengthens eyesight, detoxifying.
Cooking time approx. 10 min
Calories p. portion: 118
2 portions
Allergens: CL

Quantity of ingredients:
Chicken yolk 1 piece / 10g. (little)
Basic recipe for a chicken soup (warming) 2 cup / 500g. (yes)
Parsley 1 table spoon / 10g. (yes)

Cooking instructions:
Cook the chicken broth according to the basic recipe.
Heat broth and bubble the egg yolk. Sprinkle the chopped parsley over it and let it rest for about 2 minutes. Drink in small sips.

9.21 Compote from apples

Apple (sweet) stops diarrhea, promotes digestion, appetizing, harmonizes the stomach. Warms stomach and spleen, improves blood circulation.
Cooking time approx. 10 min
Calories p. portion: 67
2 portions
Allergens:

Quantity of ingredients:
Apple (sweet) 1 piece / 220g. (little)
Cinnamon ground 1 pinch / 1g. (yes)
Water 1 1/2 cups / 220g. (yes)

Cooking instructions:
Cook the apples (organic) with the skin and seeds. Sprinkle with cinnamon.

9.22 Compote of local fruit and dried fruit

Promotes digestion, supports urination, stops diarrhea, promotes digestion, appetizing, relieves diarrhea. Warms stomach and spleen, improves blood circulation.
Cooking time approx. 15 min
Calories p. portion: 45
4 portions
Allergens:

Quantity of ingredients:
Apple (sweet) 1 piece / 150g. (little)
Water 2 cup / 500g. (yes)
Pear 1 piece / 150g. (yes)
Cinnamon ground 1 pinch / 0,2g. (yes)
Lemon peel 1/2 teaspoon / 2g. (little)

Cooking instructions:
Cook the apple and pear with the dried fruit until soft. Sprinkle with cinnamon and lemon zest (organic).

9.23 Compote of pears

Pear benefits digestion, supports urination. Cocoa forces liver, strengthens the muscles, strengthens the defense. Good to fight fungi infections.
Cooking time approx. 10 min
Calories p. portion: 122
4 portions
Allergens:

Quantity of ingredients:
Pear 4 pieces / 800g. (yes)
Cocoa 1 pinch / 1g. (little)
Vanilla pod 1 pinch / 1g. (yes)
Anise (Common Fennel) 1/2 teaspoon / 1g. (yes)
Water 1 cup / 280g. (yes)

Cooking instructions:
Boil pears (organic - with peel), aniseed, vanilla, chili soft. Sprinkle with cocoa.

9.24 Corn coffee with cardamom

Diuretic, forcing spleen, supports urination, relaxes, reduces fat.
Cooking time approx. 5 min
Calories p. portion: 3
1 portions
Allergens:

Quantity of ingredients:
Cardamom 2 cores / 1g. (recommended)
Cereal coffee 1 table spoon / 15g. (yes)
Water 1 cup / 120g. (yes)

Cooking instructions:
Boil water, coffee, sugar and cardamom. Let it set for one min before drinking.

9.25 Couscous Salad

prevents cancer, forcing spleen, promotes digestion, stimulates liver function, reduces blood pressure, strengthens immune system, reduces radiation damage, diuretic.
Cooking time approx. 25 min
Calories p. portion: 338
3 portions
Allergens: A

Quantity of ingredients:
Peppermint 3 twigs / 30g. (yes)
Couscous 5/8 oz / 200g. (yes)
Parsley 1 Bunch / 100g. (yes)
Carrot 1/4 lbs - 4oz / 100g. (recommended)
Cucumber 1/4 lbs - 4oz / 100g. (yes)
Tomato 2 pieces / 80g. (yes)
Lemon juice 2 table spoons / 30g. (little)
Chives 1 Bunch / 100g. (little)
Water 1 cup / 100g. (yes)
Olive oil 1 table spoon / 15g. (little)
Lemon peel 1 teaspoon / 2g. (little)

Cooking instructions:
Boil in a small saucepan 250 ml. water with salt and 1 tablespoon olive oil. Add the couscous, take the stove in the front and let it swell covered for 5 minutes. Put the couscous back on the stove and let it simmer for about 2 minutes with gentle stirring. If necessary, add 1 - 3 tbsp of hot water.
Mix the couscous with lemon juice, chopped lemon peel and 1 tbsp oil, season with salt and pepper and leave to set.
Add couscous with tomatoes, cucumber, parsley (all diced), carrots (grated), chives and mint (finely chopped).
Season the couscous salad with lemon juice, salt and pepper.

9.26 Cranberry juice

Antibacterial, good to fight loss of appetite, arteriosclerosis, bladder infections, diarrhea, colds. Antipyretic, against free radicals, gout, diuretic, stomach ulcers, oral mucosa inflammation, rheumatism.
Cooking time approx. 5 min
Calories p. portion: 43
1 portions
Allergens:

Quantity of ingredients:
Water 1 cup / 125g. (yes)
Cranberries 2 table spoons / 25g. (yes)
Honey 1 table spoon / 10g. (little)

Cooking instructions:
Mix the cranberries with a little water with the blender to a pulp. Add the remaining water and sweeten with the honey.

9.27 Grated apple

Eat 3 times a day - Apple (sour) scraped and brown is stuffing. Relieves diarrhea.
Cooking time approx. 10 min
Calories p. portion: 120
1 portions
Allergens:

Quantity of ingredients:
Apple (sour) 1 piece / 200g. (little)

Cooking instructions:
Peel apple and grate as fine as possible. Leave for at least 5 minutes until it turns brown.

9.28 Grated carrots with apple

Promotes spleen and liver, reduces blood pressure, strengthens immune system, prevents cancer, reduces radiation damage, stopps diarrhea, promotes digestion, appetizing, harmonizes the stomach.
Cooking time approx. 10 min
Calories p. portion: 74
1 portions
Allergens:

Quantity of ingredients:
Carrot 1/4 lbs - 4oz / 100g. (recommended)
Lemon juice 2 teaspoons / 3g. (little)
Sugar substitute (sweetener) 1g. Or 0,034oz / 1g. (little)
Apple (sweet) 1 piece / 50g. (little)

Cooking instructions:
Mix lemon juice with sweetener. Grate the washed, thinly peeled carrots and the apple piece into the sauce and mix.

9.29 Hearty polenta mash

Strengths spleen and stomach, promotes watering, promotes digestion, detoxifying, promotes perspiration, reduces blood lipids, stimulates, dissolves stagnation, stimulates appetite, dissolves stagnation.
Cooking time approx. 10 min
Calories p. portion: 262
2 portions
Allergens:

Quantity of ingredients:
Corn Grease (Polenta) 1 cup / 120g. (yes)
Ginger fresh 1/2 teaspoon / 2g. (yes)
Water 1 1/2 cups / 240g. (yes)
Onion (spring onion) 2 pieces / 40g. (little)
Turmeric (yellow root) 1 pinch / 1g. (recommended)
Salt 1 pinch / 1g. (little)
Olive oil 1 table spoon / 10g. (little)
Nutmeg 1 pinch / 1g. (yes)

Cooking instructions:
Stir in the polenta in boiling water and let it swell for 7 min. Add green onion, grated ginger, turmeric, nutmeg, salt and olive oil and wait for 3 more minutes.

9.30 Miso soup with tofu

Vitamins, minerals and secondary plant active ingredients, invigorating, detoxifying, strengthens immune system, promotes digestion, forcing spleen, containing enzymes, reduces flatulence, alginic acid detoxifies the bowel, dissolves stagnation.
Cooking time approx. 5 min
Calories p. portion: 51
3 portions
Allergens: E

Quantity of ingredients:
Onion (spring onion) 1/2 teaspoon / 6g. (little)
Soy sauce 1 dash / 3g. (little)
Water 2 cup / 500g. (yes)

Wakame 1 piece / 5g. (yes)
Miso 3-4 table spoons / 30g. (yes)
Soy Tofu 1/8 lbs - 2oz / 50g. (yes)

Cooking instructions:
Boil soybean seedlings, wakame algae and diced tofu for 5 minutes.
Put the miso paste in the soup plate and slowly pour over the soup.
Season with Tamari sauce. Sprinkle with cutted spring onion.

9.31 Month porridge - also for babies from 7th month

Promotes spleen and liver, strengthens immune system, improves
digestion, regenerates skin, supports urination, strengthens the
muscles, tendons and bones.
Cooking time approx. 2 hours and more
Calories p. portion: 157
20 portions
Allergens:

Quantity of ingredients:
Beef soup meat 2,2 lbs / 1000g. (yes)
Carrot (Early Carrot) 7 lbs / 3000g. (recommended)
Potato 50 OZ / 1500g. (recommended)
Fennel seeds ground 1 teaspoon / 3g. (yes)
Water 3,3 lbs / 1400g. (yes)

Cooking instructions:
Wash the beef and place in the pressure cooker with about 1/2 liter of
water.
Add the fennel seeds, close the pot and put it on. Cook at level 1 in
about 45 minutes. Then remove from the heat and wait until the
pressure has dropped. (Cook in a normal saucepan for approx. 1 ½
hours) In the meantime, wash the potatoes and place them in a
saucepan without peeling. Add about 5 cm of water, bring to the boil
and cook the potatoes on a low heat for 35-40 minutes. Remove the
meat from the broth and cut into cubes of about 2 cm. Wash, clean,
peel and divide the carrots into large pieces. Cook half of the carrots in
a closed pot on level 1 in about 6 minutes. Let evaporate and lift the
carrots out with a slotted spoon. Then cook the remaining carrots. In a
bowl, finely puree the meat with carrots and 1 trowel of bouillon with the
blender until everything is chopped up.
Peel the still hot potatoes and press in portions through the potato
press. Do not crush with blenders - then the puree becomes paste-like.

Mix the loose potato puree with the carrot and meat sauce. In freezer bags, weigh 190-220 g portions (depending on age and appetite), seal and freeze in the freezer.

The porridge is stable for up to 2 months. If necessary, thaw the bag and its contents in warm water. Bring the vegetables to the boil and mix on the plate with 1 tablespoon of butter or germ oil (change daily). Add the fat after cooking - otherwise important vitamins and fatty acids will be destroyed!

9.32 Nettle-chard soup

Nettle promotes urination, detoxifies, supporting prostate disorders, reduces inflammation, analgesic. Chard supports intestinal activity, cleans intestine.
Cooking time approx. 30 min
Calories p. portion: 52
4 portions
Allergens:

Quantity of ingredients:
Olive oil 1 table spoon / 10g. (little)
Water 2 cup / 400g. (yes)
Salt 1 pinch / 1g. (little)
Chard 1 lbs / 500g. (yes)
Nettles Handful / 10g. (yes)
Pepper (ground) 1 pinch / 0,5g. (little)

Cooking instructions:
Heat the oil in a saucepan, add the washed and finely chopped Swiss chard. Salt and let simmer for 10 minutes.
Add the chopped nettles and cook for another 10 minutes. Add pepper and puree.

9.33 Noodle soup - Also for babies from 10 month

Protects the digestive system. Detoxifying, affects anorexia, reduces blood pressure, strengthens immune system, strengthens the muscles, tendons and bones. stimulates liver function, detoxifying.
Cooking time approx. 1 1/2 hours
Calories p. portion: 237
8 portions
Allergens: ACEGL

Quantity of ingredients:
Tomato paste 1 table spoon / 10g. (yes)
Celery sticks 1 bunch / 200g. (yes)
Carrot 3/4 lbs / 300g. (recommended)
Bay leaf 1 piece / 1g. (yes)
Water 4 cup / 900g. (yes)
Cauliflower 3/4 lbs / 300g. (yes)
Soy sauce 1 table spoon / 8g. (little)
Salt 1 teaspoon / 2g. (little)
Beef soup meat 3/4 lbs / 300g. (yes)
Butter Bio 1 table spoon / 10g. (little)
Noodles (wheat) with egg 3/4 lbs / 300g. (yes)
Parsley 1 Bunch / 100g. (yes)

Cooking instructions:
Simmer the meat and bay leaf in the water over low heat for about 30 minutes.
Peel and slice the carrots.
From the celery plant separate the lower end and the leaves. Wash the stems, peel off the tough threads and cut the stems into slices about 1 cm thick.
Wash the Brussels sprouts, clean them and cut the roses from below crosswise.
Wash and chop the parsley.

Add the Brussels sprouts and carrot slices to the soup and cook for about 30 minutes.

After about 10 minutes, add the celery and green leaves and the pasta. Finally, remove the bay leaf and celery green.

(For the baby, remove about 200-250 g of carrots, celery and noodles with broth, squeeze about 35 g of meat finely and add to the baby soup, stir in the butter and 1 teaspoon of chopped parsley.)

Season the remaining soup with the salt, the soy sauce, the tomato paste and the remaining parsley. Lift out the meat. Remove fat and bones and dice the meat. Serve in the soup.

9.34 Noodles with Vegetable and tomato sauce

Protects the digestive system. Detoxifying, Good to fight loss of appetite, flatulence, inflammatory bowel disease, obesity, gout, stomach ulcers, stomach cramps, rheumatism, heartburn, twelffinger intestinal ulcers, promotes digestion, helps to digest fat.
Cooking time approx. 45 min
Calories p. portion: 562
2 portions
Allergens: ACG

Quantity of ingredients:
Crème fraiche cheese 2 table spoons / 30g. (little)
Tomato 1/4 lbs - 4oz / 125g. (yes)
Carrot 1 piece / 80g. (recommended)
Zucchini 1 piece / 80g. (recommended)
Olive oil 1 table spoon / 15g. (little)
Onion (shallot) 1 piece / 20g. (little)
Oregano dried 1 pinch / 1g. (yes)
Salt 1 pinch / 1g. (little)
Pepper (ground) 1 pinch / 0,2g. (little)
Olive oil 1 table spoon / 10g. (little)
Noodles (wheat) with egg 5/8 oz / 200g. (yes)

Cooking instructions:
Boil the tomatoes with a little water, drain and collect the juice, cut the tomatoes into pieces.
Roughly grate zucchini and carrot. Heat olive oil in a pot. Steam shallots very soft. Add tomatoes, season with oregano, salt and pepper. Simmer tomatoes to a thick sauce.
Bring plenty of salted water to boil, cook the wholegrain noodles until firm.
In the cooking time of the pasta, heat in a pan olive oil. Fry the carrots while stirring, lightly salt. Add zucchini, sauté briefly while stirring. The vegetables should be soft with a bite.
Drain pasta, mix with crème fraiche, season with salt and pepper. Garnish with the tomato sauce.

9.35 Oat Congee

Strengthens immune system.
Cooking time approx. 2-4 hours
Calories p. portion: 162
3 portions
Allergens: A

Quantity of ingredients:
Water 6 cups / 700g. (yes)
Oat 1 cup / 125g. (yes)

Cooking instructions:
Cook oats and water in a ratio of about 1: 6. The amount of water determines the thickness of the mash (pure matter of taste). The oats swell, so do not take much. Put the oats in a saucepan with good insulation and a heavy lid. It is important to simmer the oats after a short boil on the slightest flame, otherwise it burns. Cook the oat for 2-4 hours. The longer it cooks, the more he strengthens.

9.36 Oatmeal soup with spring onion and carrots

Reduces blood pressure, strengthens immune system, prevents cancer, reduces radiation damage, stimulates digestion, reduces pain, stimulates appetite, dissolves stagnation.
Cooking time approx. 30 min
Calories p. portion: 135
3 portions
Allergens: AG

Quantity of ingredients:
Nutmeg 1 pinch / 1g. (yes)
Onion (spring onion) 2 pieces / 40g. (little)
Water 2 cup / 480g. (yes)
Lovage 1 stem / 15g. (yes)
Carrot 2 pieces / 200g. (recommended)
Oat 6 table spoons / 48g. (yes)
Butter Bio 1 table spoon / 15g. (little)

Cooking instructions:
Roast the oats in butter, add salt and spices, pour in water and heat till it boils. After 10 min. add the grated carrots and lovage, cook for 10 minutes. Finely add chopped onion.

9.37 Polenta with peach

Relieves fatigue, forcing spleen, diuretic, strengthens the defense, good to fight fungi infections, lets urine and bile juice flow, prevents the aging process, strengthens brain cells.
Cooking time approx. 20 min
Calories p. portion: 197
3 portions
Allergens:

Quantity of ingredients:
Cinnamon ground 1 pinch / 1g. (yes)
Peaches 2-3 pieces / 400g. (little)
Vanilla pod 1 pinch / 1g. (yes)
Corn Grease (Polenta) 1 cup / 120g. (yes)
Water 1 1/2 cups / 240g. (yes)

Cooking instructions:
Pour the polenta into a pan of hot water with constant stirring until the polenta has the desired consistency. Pull the polenta from the fire and let it soak for 10 minutes.

Wash fresh peaches and cut into quarters. Pour into the finished polenta the peaches, add the vanilla and add Chili to taste, stir and let it go for 3 minutes.

Winter varieties: Pickled fruit, pear, apples

9.38 Potato gnocchi with vegetables and basil sauce

Strengthens immune system, promotes weight loss. Good to fight immunodeficiency, loss of appetite, flatulence, high blood pressure. Relaxing and reassuring.
Cooking time approx. 1 hour
Calories p. portion: 167
4 portions
Allergens: ACGL

Quantity of ingredients:
Salt 1 pinch / 1g. (little)
Basic recipe for a vegetable soup (nutritious) 1 cup / 250g. (yes)
Wheat flour 1 oz / 25g. (yes)
Chicken yolk 1 piece / 20g. (little)
Nutmeg 1 pinch / 0,2g. (yes)

Wheat semolina 1/2 oz / 15g. (yes)
Salt 1 pinch / 1g. (little)
Crème fraiche cheese 1 table spoon / 20g. (little)
Celery root 1/8 lbs - 2oz / 50g. (yes)
Pepper (ground) 1 pinch / 0,2g. (little)
Carrot 1/4 lbs - 4oz / 100g. (recommended)
Zucchini 1/4 lbs - 4oz / 100g. (recommended)
Cauliflower 1/4 lbs - 4oz / 100g. (yes)
Broccoli 1/4 lbs - 4oz / 100g. (yes)
Potato 5/8 lbs - 8oz / 250g. (recommended)
Lemon peel 1/2 teaspoon / 2g. (little)
Basil (fresh) 1 Bunch / 125g. (yes)
Ginger fresh 1/2 teaspoon / 2g. (yes)
Nutmeg 1 pinch / 0,2g. (yes)

Cooking instructions:
Steam the potatoes gently, peel and pass hot through the potato press.
Process the hot potatoes with flour, semolina, egg, nutmeg and salt to a
smooth dough. Let dough rest for 3o minutes.
Make small rolls (2 cm) out of the dough with flour-dusted hands, cut off
1 cm thin slices. To create the typical gnocchi shape, gently dab the
dough pieces with your thumb. Leave the gnocchi in lightly boiling
salted water for 6 - 8 minutes. Lift the gnocchi out of the pot with the
skimmer.

Heat the vegetable stock till it boils. Add diced celery, grated lemon
peel, finely chopped ginger and 1 pinch of nutmeg. Cover and simmer
for about 10 minutes. Using the blender, puree the vegetable broth,
celery, chopped basil and crème fraiche into a smooth sauce. Season
with salt and nutmeg.

Cut carrots, zucchini, cauliflower and broccoli into small pieces and
cook covered in a sieve over steam for 8 minutes until firm.
Heat the sauce again and add to the vegetables and arrange over the
gnocchi.

9.39 Potato with dandelion salad

Promotes spleen, reduces inflammation, improves digestion,
regenerates skin, supports urinating, lowers cholesterol, detoxifying,
reduces inflammation, forcing spleen and digestive system, detoxifying,
dissolves

Cooking time approx. 25 min
Calories p. portion: 162
2 portions
Allergens:

Quantity of ingredients:
Onion white 1/2 piece / 20g. (little)
Salt 1 pinch / 1g. (little)
Potato 5/8 lbs - 8oz / 250g. (recommended)
Pepper white (ground) 1 pinch / 0,5g. (little)
Sunflower oil 1 table spoon / 10g. (little)
Dandelion (young plants) 1/4 lbs - 4oz / 125g. (yes)

Cooking instructions:
Cook the potatoes in salted water and cut into thin slices. Finely chop
the onion. Now season the potatoes with oil, salt and pepper and add
the dandelion and mix.

9.40 Potato-basil soup

Reduces inflammation, improves digestion, supports urination, lowers
cholesterol, reduces blood pressure, strengthens immune system,
prevents cancer, reduces radiation damage, antioxidativ, dissolves
stagnation.
Cooking time approx. 25 min
Calories p. portion: 96
4 portions
Allergens: L

Quantity of ingredients:
Basil (fresh) 1 Bunch / 50g. (yes)
Carrot 2 pieces / 100g. (recommended)
Salt 1 pinch / 1g. (little)
Peppers powder 1 pinch / 1g. (little)
Sugar cane sugar 1 pinch / 1g. (little)
Potato 4 pieces / 200g. (recommended)
Pepper (ground) 1 pinch / 0,5g. (little)
Water 2 cups / 450g. (yes)
Olive oil 1 table spoon / 10g. (little)
Garlic 1 clove / 3g. (little)
Lemon 1 teaspoon / 3g. (little)
Celery root 1 piece / 500g. (yes)
Ground 1 pinch / 1g. (yes)

Cooking instructions:
Peeled and chopped 4 medium potatoes in a pot of hot water and 2 chopped medium carrots, a piece of celery root, a pinch of pepper, a pinch of ground cumin, crushed a small clove of garlic, a pinch of salt, 1 teaspoon of lemon juice, simmer until the Vegetables is soft.

Add 1 bunch finely chopped basil into one half of the soup and puree everything; stir in the other half of the basil; with rose paprika, a pinch of whole cane sugar, 1 tablespoon of olive oil or butter, freshly ground pepper, salt to taste.

9.41 Pumpkin soup

Promotes digestion, forcing spleen and stomach, reduces blood pressure, strengthens immune system, prevents cancer, reduces radiation damage, improves digestion, regenerates skin, lowers cholesterol, reduces blood glucose, protects liver.
Cooking time approx. 1 hour
Calories p. portion: 105
3 portions
Allergens:

Quantity of ingredients:
Potato 2 pieces / 120g. (recommended)
Anise (Common Fennel) 1 pinch / 1g. (yes)
Parsley 1 table spoon / 7g. (yes)
Water 1 cup / 120g. (yes)
Onion white 1 piece / 50g. (little)
Carrot 2 pieces / 100g. (recommended)
Pumpkin 3/4 lbs / 300g. (yes)
Olive oil 1 table spoon / 10g. (little)
Salt 1 pinch / 1g. (little)

Cooking instructions:
Add the olive oil to the pan, add the diced pumpkin, diced carrots and potatoes. Roast them shortly, add the finely chopped onion, fill with water, add enough water to cover the vegetables at least 3 finger-widths. Boil at low heat.
Season with sea salt, add small cutted parsley, a pinch of anise (little). Allow to simmer for about 35 minutes. Then purée the soup and add some water, depending on the consistency of the soup.

9.42 Puréed banana

Eat 2 times a day, regulates gastrointestinal function.
Cooking time approx. 7 min
Calories p. portion: 144
1 portions
Allergens:

Quantity of ingredients:
Banana 1 piece / 150g. (recommended)

Cooking instructions:
Mix the banana with the fork or purée with a blender. Leave to brown for at least 5 minutes.

9.43 Quick zucchini soup

Diuretic, supports urination. Strengthens gastrointestinal function, expands blood vessels, prevents cancer, prevents diseases (in the elderly). Stimulates liver function, detoxifying.
Cooking time approx. 10 min
Calories p. portion: 42
4 portions
Allergens:

Quantity of ingredients:
Chives 1 teaspoon / 3g. (little)
Parsley 1 table spoon / 7g. (yes)
Corn germ oil 2 table spoons / 6g. (little)
Onion white 1 piece / 50g. (little)
Water 2 cup / 400g. (yes)
Zucchini 2-3 pieces / 500g. (recommended)

Cooking instructions:
Fry chopped onion in oil. Add sliced zucchini and sauté well. Pour with water. Chop parsley and chives, add and puree everything.

9.44 Rice congee with carrots and fennel

Worms, forcing spleen, relieves constipation, stimulates nerves, detoxifying, reduces inflammation, improves blood circulation, reduces blood pressure, strengthens immune system, prevents cancer, reduces radiation

Cooking time approx. 2 hours and more
Calories p. portion: 131
3 portions
Allergens: G

Quantity of ingredients:
Fennel 1 piece / 250g. (yes)
Basic recipe for a rice soup (Congee) 2 cup / 500g. (yes)
Carrot 2 pieces / 100g. (recommended)
Butter Bio 1 teaspoon / 3g. (little)
Cardamom 1/2 teaspoon / 1g. (recommended)

Cooking instructions:
Cook rice congee according to basic recipe.
Clean and cut carrots and fennel.

When carrots and fennel are cooked from the beginning, they serve wholesomeness. If added shortly before the end of the cooking time, taste and vitamins are retained.
Refine with butter and cardamom before serving.

9.45 Rice with parsnips

Rich in vitamins, minerals potassium and zinc. Good to fight blood circulation disorders, thrombose, risk of embolism, high blood pressure, a headache, heart attack and stroke, yeast infections.
Cooking time approx. 45 min
Calories p. portion: 206
3 portions
Allergens:

Quantity of ingredients:
Olive oil 1 table spoon / 10g. (little)
Sage 1 teaspoon / 3g. (yes)
Water 1 1/2 cups / 200g. (yes)
Salt 1 pinch / 1g. (little)
Parsnip 3-4 pieces / 450g. (yes)
Rice variety any 1 cup / 120g. (yes)

Cooking instructions:
Peel the parsnips and cut into slices. Fry for a short time in oil. Add the rice and fry again for a short time. Add the water and cook it at least 30 min. Sprinkle with fresh chopped sage.

9.46 Rice with stewed vegetables

Reduces blood pressure, strengthens immune system, prevents cancer, reduces radiation damage, extremely low fat content, good to fight blood circulation disorders, thrombose, risk of embolism, a headache, heart attack and stroke. Is diuretic.
Cooking time approx. 20 min
Calories p. portion: 166
2 portions
Allergens: L

Quantity of ingredients:
Champignon 1/2 cup / 50g. (little)
Water 1/2 cup / 0g. (yes)
Linseed oil 1 dash / 3g. (little)
Carrot 2 pieces / 180g. (recommended)
Lemon peel 1 piece / 3g. (little)
Rice variety any 1/2 cup / 60g. (yes)
Celery sticks 1/2 piece / 5g. (yes)
Cress 2 table spoons / 20g. (yes)
Water 3 cups / 300g. (yes)

Cooking instructions:
Cook rice according to basic recipe with a piece of lemon peel.
Steam chopped carrots, celery and mushrooms until soft.
Then sprinkle with cress. Then add a dash of high quality cold oil.

9.47 Roasted barley patties

Improves digestion, lowers cholesterol, good to fight diarrhea, ulceration, joint pain, stomach problems. Promotes spleen and liver, reduces blood pressure, strengthens immune system, prevents cancer, reduces radiation damage, stimulates liver function.
Cooking time approx. 1 1/2 hours
Calories p. portion: 398
3 portions
Allergens: ACN

Quantity of ingredients:
Lemon 1/2 piece / 15g. (little)
Pepper (ground) 1 pinch / 0,5g. (little)
Potato 1 piece / 140g. (recommended)
Carrot 1 piece / 120g. (recommended)
Champignon 2-3 pieces / 25g. (little)

Salt 1 pinch / 1g. (little)
Barley grouts 1 cup / 120g. (yes)
Onion white 1 piece / 50g. (little)
Water 1 1/2 cups / 250g. (yes)
Peppers powder 1 pinch / 1g. (little)
Sesame oil 2 table spoons / 50g. (little)
Bread roll 1 piece / 35g. (yes)
Parsley 2 table spoons / 15g. (yes)
Chicken egg 1 piece / 55g. (little)
Ginger fresh 1/2 teaspoon / 1g. (yes)

Cooking instructions:
Preparation:
Place 2 large cups of hot water in a saucepan; add 1 large cup of barley porridge; simmer for 2 minutes while stirring; then let it swell for 20 minutes on the switched off stove; take down and let cool.
Cook in boiling water 1 large potato, chopped and cut.
Soak 1 roll in hot water and squeeze well.
Then: Mix the barley groats and crushed the potato. Add 1 grated carrot, 2 - 3 chopped mushrooms, 1 egg, 1 finely chopped onion, 1/2 teaspoon grated ginger, a pinch of pepper, a pinch of salt, a little lemon juice, chopped parsley, plenty of rose paprika; knead well and form patties; heat sesame oil in a hot pan; fry the patties for about 15 minutes over a gentle heat; turn at half time.

Also fits well: lettuce, soybean vegetables.

9.48 Roasted millet with Celery sticks

Promotes spleen and kidney, diuretic, promoting metabolism.
Cooking time approx. 30 min
Calories p. portion: 400
2 portions
Allergens: L

Quantity of ingredients:
Cress 1 teaspoon / 3g. (yes)
Water 1 1/2 cups / 240g. (yes)
Millet 1 cup / 120g. (yes)
Celery sticks 2 rods / 50g. (yes)
Herbs various 1 table spoon / 10g. (yes)
Water 2 table spoons / 30g. (yes)

Salt 1 pinch / 1g. (little)
Sage 3-4 leaves / 2g. (yes)

Cooking instructions:
Roast millet briefly, pour over water, heat till it boils and let stand for 20 min. to swell.
Cut celery into small pieces and mix with water, salt and fresh herbs and cook for 10 min. Add to the millet.
Sprinkle fresh sage or watercress over it.

9.49 Roasted millet with plum compote

Supports urination, promotes spleen and kidney, strengthens the defense. Good to fight fungi infections.
Cooking time approx. 30 min
Calories p. portion: 139
4 portions
Allergens:

Quantity of ingredients:
Acerola fruit nectar or powder 1/2 teaspoon / 1g. (little)
Water 5/8 lbs - 8oz / 250g. (yes)
Millet 1 cup / 120g. (yes)
Water 1 1/2 cups / 250g. (yes)
Cinnamon ground 1 pinch / 1g. (yes)
Vanilla pod 1 pinch / 1g. (yes)
Plum 1 1/2 cups / 250g. (little)

Cooking instructions:
Roast millet briefly, pour over water, heat till it boils and let stand for 20 min. to swell.
Cook plums with water, vanilla and cinnamon 10 min. then strain. Add acerola and add to the millet.

9.50 Rosemary Potatoes

Reduces Inflammation, improves digestion, regenerates skin, supports urination, lowers cholesterol. Rosemary stimulates digestion, strengthens lung, promotes spleen and kidney, dries out.
Cooking time approx. 30 min
Calories p. portion: 188
2 portions
Allergens:

Quantity of ingredients:
Potato 6-8 pieces / 420g. (recommended)
Rosemary 1 teaspoon / 2g. (yes)
Olive oil 1 table spoon / 10g. (little)
Salt (herbal) 1 pinch / 1g. (little)

Cooking instructions:
Cut the potatoes into halfs, apply a little olive oil on the cut surface, then salt, sprinkle 2 - 3 rosemary needles on the potatoes.
Place the potatoes on the baking tray and bake them in the preheated oven for approx. 25 minutes to 190°C/374°F.

9.51 Semolina dumpling soup

Reduces blood pressure, strengthens immune system, prevents cancer, reduces radiation damage, dissolves stagnation, promotes weight loss. Good to fight immunodeficiency, loss of appetite, flatulence, high blood pressure, depressions, diabetes, diarrhea.
Cooking time approx. 1 hour
Calories p. portion: 287
3 portions
Allergens: ACGLO

Quantity of ingredients:
Wheat semolina 3 oz / 80g. (yes)
Chives 1 table spoon / 10g. (little)
Nutmeg 1 pinch / 1g. (yes)
Pepper (ground) 1 pinch / 0,5g. (little)
Chicken egg 1 piece / 65g. (little)
Basic recipe for a beef soup (warming) 2 cup / 500g. (little)
Salt 1 pinch / 1g. (little)
Parsley 1 table spoon / 10g. (yes)
Butter Bio 1/8 lbs - 2oz / 40g. (little)

Cooking instructions:
Knead the ingredients for the dumplings to a firm dough and allow to swell for 30 minutes. Heat the broth (basic recipe for a beef broth warming). Then cut out with a spoon dumplings, place in the prepared broth and let stand for 20 minutes. Before serving, chop parsley and sprinkle with thinly sliced chives.

9.52 Supplementary nutrition

Protein-rich drink with very high energy density. Optimized protein content balances nitrogen losses and promotes protein anabolism.
Cooking time approx. 5 min
Calories p. portion: 1045
1 portions
Allergens:

Quantity of ingredients:
Supplementary nutrition 1 package / 250g. (yes)

Cooking instructions:
Use only as directed by the physician or therapist.

9.53 Tea Black tea (Russian tea)

Black tea improves blood circulation.
Cooking time approx. 10 min
Calories p. portion: 7
1 portions
Allergens:

Quantity of ingredients:
Black tea 1 table spoon / 5g. (recommended)
Water 1 cup / 120g. (yes)

Cooking instructions:
For each cup you use a teaspoonful or a teabag.
Pour green tea only with 60 to 80 ° C / 140 to 176 °F hot water, otherwise it will be bitter.
If the tea has a stimulating effect, let it draw for two to three minutes. It has a calming effect for a duration of five minutes (no longer, otherwise it will be bitter!).
Another method: Pour the tea leaves with about 70 ° C / 158 °F hot water and pour the water immediately again.
Then just pour hot water again. The bitter substances disappear and the tea gets a milder aroma.

9.54 Tea from anise

Anise (wild fennel) promotes digestion, forcing spleen and stomach.
Cooking time approx. 15 min
Calories p. portion: 3
4 portions
Allergens:

Quantity of ingredients:
Anise (Common Fennel) 1 teaspoon / 3g. (yes)
Water 2 cup / 500g. (yes)

Cooking instructions:
Heat the water till it boils and put it aside. Add anise.
10 min. to let go.
Pour through a tea strainer. Sweet to taste with honey.

In order to achieve a salutary effect, you should drink 2 cups of anise
tea per day.

9.55 Tea from blue mallow

Good to fight stomach pain, gastritis.
Cooking time approx. 10 min
Calories p. portion: 0
2 portions
Allergens:

Quantity of ingredients:
Blue mallow tee 2 table spoons / 14g. (recommended)
Water 2 cup / 500g. (yes)

Cooking instructions:
Heat the water till it boils and put it aside. Add cheesecloth tea and 10
min. to let go. Sweet to taste with honey.
Strain when pouring.

9.56 Tea from catuaba

A high proportion of minerals and trace elements. Especially magnesium, potassium and calcium are obtained in considerable quantities. Catuaba is refreshing.
Cooking time approx. 20 min
Calories p. portion: 6
2 portions
Allergens:

Quantity of ingredients:
Honey 1 teaspoon / 3g. (little)
Water 2 cup / 500g. (yes)
Lemon juice 1/2 teaspoon / 2g. (little)
Catuaba tea 2-3 teaspoon / 5g. (yes)

Cooking instructions:
Boil a heaped tablespoon of tea for about 5 minutes in ½ liter of water and then leave for about 15 minutes. Sweet with honey. A small splash of lemon juice added to the tea during infusion helps to optimally dissolve the minerals.

9.57 Tea from chamomile

Good to fight flatulence, nausea, intestinal cramps, diarrhea, inflammation of the oral mucosa, influenza infections, stomach and intestinal mucosa infections, badly healing wounds, nausea, colds, skin rashes, inflammation in the genital and anal area.
Cooking time approx. 10 min
Calories p. portion: 0
1 portions
Allergens:

Quantity of ingredients:
Water 1 cup / 120g. (yes)
Chamomile 1 teaspoon / 3g. (yes)

Cooking instructions:
Heat the water till it boils and put it aside. Chamomile flowers added and 10 min. to let go.

9.58 Tender fennel vegetables

Relieves constipation, stimulates nerves, reduces inflammation, improves blood circulation, regenerates skin, supports urination. Promotes digestion.
Cooking time approx. 25 min
Calories p. portion: 70
2 portions
Allergens: G

Quantity of ingredients:
Water 2 table spoons / 20g. (yes)
Butter Bio 1 table spoon / 10g. (little)
Fennel 1/4 lbs - 4oz / 100g. (yes)
Potato 1 piece / 50g. (recommended)

Cooking instructions:
Wash the potato and peel with a peeler. Cut into cubes of about 2 cm. Wash the fennel, remove stained, dark spots and cut the tuber. Heat till it boils with 2 tablespoons of water in a small saucepan. Cook on low heat for about 15 minutes. Fish out the caraway seeds. Puree the vegetables with the blender and stir in the butter.
Fennel and caraway soothe the stomach and prevent bloating. In addition, fennel contains a lot of vitamin C and folic acid. An ideal meal for sick children.

9.59 Tomato soup

Promotes digestion, helps to digest fat, supports urination, reduces blood pressure, dissolves stagnation. Contains unsaturated fatty acids, is antioxidativ.
Cooking time approx. 10 min
Calories p. portion: 100
2 portions
Allergens:

Quantity of ingredients:
Water 5/8 lbs - 8oz / 250g. (yes)
Onion white 1 piece / 60g. (little)
Cinnamon ground 1 pinch / 1g. (yes)
Olive oil 1 table spoon / 15g. (little)
Pepper (ground) 1 pinch / 0,5g. (little)
Peppers powder 1 pinch / 1g. (little)
Tomato 6 pieces / 250g. (yes)

Salt 1 pinch / 1g. (little)
Basil (fresh) 1 teaspoon / 2g. (yes)

Cooking instructions:
Roast the onion in a pot. Salt and spices. Briefly roast. Put washed and quartered tomatoes in the pan. Stir and sauté briefly. Add a quart of water and heat till it boils. Cook for a quarter of an hour and puree.

9.60 Vegetable bowl with tofu and curry on rice

Diuretic, reduces blood glucose. Reduces flatulence, supports digestion. Contains ideal herbal mucus, which provides regeneration of the small and large intestinal flora. Reduces blood pressure, strengthens immune
Cooking time approx. 30 min
Calories p. portion: 162
6 portions
Allergens: E

Quantity of ingredients:
Garlic 2 cloves / 3g. (little)
Pumpkin 1 piece / 400g. (yes)
Carrot 1 piece / 100g. (recommended)
Potato 1 piece / 70g. (recommended)
Turnips 2 pieces / 50g. (yes)
Olive oil 2 table spoons / 20g. (little)
Parsnip 1 piece / 150g. (yes)
Cauliflower 1/4 piece / 250g. (yes)
Sweet potato 1 piece / 70g. (recommended)
Water 2 cup / 500g. (yes)
Curry 2 table spoons / 16g. (yes)
Onion white 1 piece / 60g. (little)
Okra 12 pieces / 200g. (yes)
Soy Tofu 1 piece / 250g. (yes)
Basil 2 table spoons / 12g. (yes)
Salt 1 pinch / 0,5g. (little)
Broccoli 1/2 piece / 250g. (yes)

Cooking instructions:
Heat the oil at medium temperature in a large, heavy casserole, add the garlic and onion and sauté with constant stirring. Sprinkle curry powder over it, fry gently for about 5 minutes and make sure that the garlic and curry do not burn. Add the water and heat till it boils. Gradually peel all

vegetables, dice and add, starting with the varieties that need the longest cooking time. Once the water has boiled again, reduce the heat and simmer the vegetables for about 15 minutes. When it is almost soft. Add the cauliflower and broccoli florets and the okra and cook the stew for another 10 to 15 minutes. Add the tofu during the last 5 minutes.

Cook the brown rice at the same time: Sprinkle the rice in a medium saucepan with water, salt and cover for about 20 minutes. cook on a low heat. Take from the fire and another 10 min. to let go.

Arrange the stew over the brown rice and sprinkle with basil.

9.61 Vegetable miso soup with tofu

Very powerful, strengthens after febrile illness, reduces blood pressure, strengthens immune system, prevents cancer, reduces radiation damage, improves blood circulation, strengthens liver and kidney, detoxifying, strengthens the muscles, reduces flatulence, forcing spleen.
Cooking time approx. 15 min
Calories p. portion: 107
4 portions
Allergens: EN

Quantity of ingredients:
Leek 2 inches / 10g. (little)
Soy Tofu 2 table spoons / 30g. (yes)
Endive salad 2 table spoons / 30g. (yes)
Carrot 1 piece / 70g. (recommended)
Water 3 cups / 750g. (yes)
Onion (shallot) 1 piece / 20g. (little)
Sesame oil 2 table spoons / 35g. (little)
Miso 2 table spoons / 15g. (yes)
Ginger fresh 1/2 teaspoon / 1g. (yes)

Cooking Instructions:
In sesame oil first sauté onions, then carrots and a little leek; Pour in water and simmer gently; add the bean sprouts and endive leaves and leave to stand; Tofu cubes, add a little ginger; at the end stir in a little cooled cooking-water the Miso.

9.62 Yellow lentil soup

Strengthens heart and kidney, diuretic, promotes spleen, calms the stomach, promotes digestion, strengthens immune system, prevents cancer, reduces radiation damage, stimulates liver function, antioxidativ.
Cooking time approx. 20 min
Calories p. portion: 155
7 portions
Allergens: A

Quantity of ingredients:
Lentils yellow 1 lbs / 500g. (little)
Onion white 1 piece / 50g. (little)
Water 4 cup / 1000g. (yes)
Turmeric (yellow root) 1 pinch / 1g. (recommended)
Cardamom 1 pinch / 1g. (recommended)
Salt 1 pinch / 1g. (little)
Olive oil 1 table spoon / 10g. (little)
Carrot 2 pieces / 150g. (recommended)
Kohlrabi 1 piece / 300g. (little)
Parsley 1/2 bunch / 100g. (yes)
Lemon juice 1/2 piece / 15g. (little)
White bread (wheat bread) 7 slices / 140g. (yes)

Cooking instructions:
Wash lenses well in a colander. Heat oil in a pot. Add finely chopped onion, sliced carrots, diced kohlrabi and spices, sauté and salt. Add the lentils and cover with water and simmer for 20 minutes. Add water as needed and season with salt. Sprinkle with fresh parsley or fresh green cilantro and drizzle with lemon juice.
Here you can also use red lenses. (same cooking time).
Serve with white bread.

9.63 Zucchini semolina cream soup

Good to fight loss of appetite, reduces blood pressure, promotes weight loss. Good to fight loss of appetite, flatulence, inflammatory bowel disease, rheumatism, heartburn.
Cooking time approx. 25 min
Calories p. portion: 146
4 portions
Allergens: AGL

Quantity of ingredients:
Lovage 1/2 teaspoon / 2g. (yes)
Nutmeg 1 pinch / 0,5g. (yes)
Anise (Common Fennel) 1 pinch / 0,5g. (yes)
Parsley 1 Bunch / 100g. (yes)
Zucchini 7/8 lbs / 400g. (recommended)
Ginger fresh 1/2 teaspoon / 1g. (yes)
Crème fraiche cheese 2 table spoons / 20g. (little)
Lemon peel 1/4 piece / 2g. (little)
Salt 1 pinch / 1g. (little)
Pepper (ground) 1 pinch / 0,5g. (little)
Wheat semolina 2 table spoons / 20g. (yes)
Butter Bio 1/2 oz / 20g. (little)
Basic recipe for a vegetable soup (nutritious) 3 1/2 cups / 800g. (yes)

Cooking instructions:
Melt the butter in a saucepan, add the semolina and fry briefly while stirring. Add half of the chopped parsley, sauté for a short time, pour vegetable broth according to the basic recipe, season with chopped lovage, nutmeg and anise. Cook the soup without lid lightly for 10 minutes. Add the finely chopped zucchini and the small piece of lemon zest, cook gently for 5 minutes until the zucchini are tender. Remove the lemon peel.
Using the blender, finely puree the soup with the crème fraiche and the remaining parsley.

10 Effects of food

10.1 Use ingredients: recommendable

Acai powder
Banana
Banana (cooking banana)
Bitter Herb liqueur
Black tea
Blackthorn (Sloe)
Blue mallow tee
Cardamom
Carrot
Carrot (Early Carrot)
Carrot juice without sugar
Channa-Dal
Chinese pearl barley
Cream 10% coffee cream
Dill

Fox nut, gorgon nut, makhana
Hibiscus
Kalmus
Kudzu
Licorice root tea
Lily bulbs
Mascarpone cheese
Potato
Potato (mealy)
Potato flour
Sweet potato
Topinambur
Turmeric (yellow root)
Zucchini

10.2 Use ingredients: yes

Agar agar (kelp)
Agrimony
Amaranth
Amaranth Pops
Angelica root
Anise (Common Fennel)
Apple puree
Arrowroot
Artichoke
Asparagus (green or white)
Aubergine
Baking powder
Balm
Banchatee (green tea)
barberry
Barley
Barley flour
Barley grass powder
Barley grouts
Barley malt
Barley not peeled
Basic recipe for a chicken soup
(warming)
Basic recipe for a rice soup (Congee)
Basic recipe for a vegetable soup
(nutritious)
Basil
Basil (fresh)
Batavia
Bay leaf
Beef fillet

Beef meat
Beef meat (calf)
Beef soup meat
Berries of the season
Berry juice
Bitter Lemon
Bitter orange peel
Black caraway
Blackberry dried (unripe fruit)
Blackberry leaves
Blackberry´s
Blueberry
Blueberry dried
Bocksdorn fruits (Fructus Lycii, Goji,
goji berry dried)
Borage
Bread roll
Bread with carob kernel flour
Breadcrumbs (wheat bread, bread roll)
Broccoli
Buckbean
Buckwheat
Buckwheat (roasted) Kasha
Bulgur (cereals)
Burdock root tea
Cantaloupe
Carambola (Star fruit)
Carob flour, St. john's bread
Cauliflower
Caviar
Celery root

Celery sticks
Cereal coffee
Chamomile
Chamomile tea
Chard
Chervil
Chervil dried
Chickweed
Chicory
Chrysanthemum blossom tea
Cinnamon ground
Cinnamon sticks
Clove
Cod
Codfish
Compote (fruits of the season)
Coriander
Coriander (fresh)
Corn
Corn (fast polenta)
Corn (roasted)
Corn flour
Corn Grease (Polenta)
Corn silk tea
Corn starch
Couscous
Crab
Cranberries
Cranberry
Cranberry juice
Cress
Crucian
Cucumber
Cucumber (bitter)
Cucumber (spicy cucumber)
Cumin (Caraway seed)
Curcuma
Currant (black)
Currant (red)
Currant (white)
Curry
Curry paste red
Daisy
Dandelion (young plants)
Dandelion juice
Dandelionroots tea
Dashi
Dulse (seaweed)
Dyer's broom herb
Elderberries
Eldorberry blossom tee
Endive salad
Fennel
Fennel seeds ground

Fennel tea
Fenugreek (Trigonella foenum-graecum)
Fig
Fig dried
Fish pieces mixed (fresh water)
Flounder
Flower pollen
Freshwater crab
Freshwater fish
Fruit tea
Garam Masala powder
Gelatin white
Gelee Royal
Gentian root
Gentian root tea
Ginger fresh
Ginger powder
Ginkgo fruit
Ginseng
Ginseng root
Gooseberry
Gourd
Grapefruit (Pomelo)
Grapefruit dried peel
Grapefruit juice
Green tea
Ground
Ground caraway
Guava
Herbal tea mix
Herbs bitter
Herbs of Provence
Herbs various
Herbs wild
Hibiscus tea
Hokkaido pumpkin
Horehound leaves
Hyssop
Iceberg lettuce
Jasmine blossoms tee
Jellyfish
Juniper berry
King Solomon's-seal
Kombu seaweed (Saccharina japonica)
Kukicha tea
Kumquats
Ladyfingers
Lamb's lettuce
Lamb's lettuce
Lavender blossoms
Leaf salads (bitter)
Lemon Balm (dried)
Lemon Balm (fresh)

Lemongrass
Lettuce
Lime blossom tea
Liver smoothing tea
Lobster
Longane
Loquate / Japanese medlar
Lotus roots
Lotus seeds
Lovage
Lovage seeds
Luo Han Guo fruit
Lychee
Lychee in Preserved
Lye roll
Mallow (Malva sylvestris) blossom tea
Malt
Mango
Maple syrup
Marjoram
Mediterranean fish (cod, plaice, haddock, sea eel, mackerel)
Medlar
Millet
Millet flakes
Miso
Miso black (fermented)
Mixed Pickles
Mulberry fruit
Mulled Wine Spice
Mussels
Mustard
Mustard Dijon
Mustard medium hot
Mustard seeds
Mustard sweet
Nasturtium (nose-twister or nose-tweaker)
Nettles
Noodles (wheat) with egg
Noodles (wheat, lasagne) with egg
Noodles (wheat, ribbon noodles) with egg
Noodles (wheat, spaghetti) with egg
Nutmeg
Oat
Oat flakes roasted
Oat flour
Oat fusion (baby food)
Oat milk
Octopus
Octopus
Okra
Orange blossom

Oregano dried
Oregano fresh
Oyster shell powder
Oysters
Papaya
Parsley
Parsley root
Parsnip
Passion blossoms tea
Passion fruit
Pear
Pear juice
Pearl barley
Pearl barley
Peppermint
Peppermint tea
Perch
Pimento
Pomegranate
Pork ham
Pork ham cooked
Pork ham smoked
Prickly pear
Pudding powder vanilla
Pumpkin
Quince
Quinoa
Radicchio
Radish leaves
Rapeseed oil
Raspberry
Raspberry dried (immature)
Raspberry leaf tea
Red beet
Red berry (without sugar)
Ribworttea
Rice (fragrance)
Rice (Gaoliang / Sorghum)
Rice flour
Rice long grain rice
Rice malt
Rice mash
Rice noodles
Rice round grain
Rice starch
Rice sticky
Rice sweet
Rice variety any
Romaine lettuce / lettuce salad
Rose blossom tea
Rose hip
Rose hip tea
Rose leaf tea
Rosemary

Rucola
Rusk
Safflower (Dyer's thistle / Hong Hua)
Saffron
Sage
Salsify
Sea buckthorn
Seacrab
Shrimp
Shrimps
Sorrel
Soy flour
Soy noodles
Soy Tofu
Soy Tofu smoked
Soybean milk
Spelled flakes
Spelled grain
Spelled semolina
Spinach
Spiny lobsters
St. Benedict's thistle, blessed thistle, holy thistle, spotted thistle
Star anise
Stevia (candyleaf, sweetleaf)
Strawberries
Supplementary nutrition
Tarragon (Estragon)
Tea mixture uric acid lowering
Thyme
Thyme dried
Tomato
Tomato juice
Tomato paste
Tomato puree
Tonic Water
Trout

Trout (smoked)
Truffle
Tsampa (roasted barley flour)
Turkey breast meat
Turnips
Umeboshi paste
Valerian
Vanilla
Vanilla pod
Vanilla powder
Vanilla sugar natural
Wakame
Water
Water hot
Watermelon
Wax gourd
Wheat flakes
Wheat flatbread/pita bread
Wheat flour
Wheat semolina
Wheat semolina for children
Wheatgrass juice
Wheatgrass powder
White bread (baguette)
White bread (pretzel sticks)
White bread (roll)
White bread (wheat bread)
White breadcrumbs
White dumpling bread (wheat bread cut into chunks)
Wild herbs
Wild strawberries
Wormwood herb
Yam root, yam root tuber
Yarrow
Yarrow tea
Yogi tea

10.3 Use ingredients: little

Acerola fruit nectar or powder
Agave nectar
Aloe juice
Apple (sour)
Apple (sweet)
Apple juice (natural cloudy)
Apricot jam
Apricot nectar
Apricots
Apricots juice
Avocado
Bamboo shoots
Basic recipe for a beef soup

Basic recipe for a beef soup (warming)
Basic recipe for a fish soup
Bean oil
Bearberry leaf
Beef meatbones
Beef Oxtail pieces
Black beans
Black fungus mushroom
Blackberry jam
Black-eyed peas
Blueberry jam
Blueberry juice
Boletus mushroom

Borage oil
Boxhorn clover seeds
Broad beans (thick beans)
Brussels sprouts
Buckwheat whole grain
Bush beans
Butter (half fat)
Butter beans white
Butter Bio
Calamari
Capers in olive oil
Champignon
Chanterelle
Chenpi (chinese tangerine bowl)
Cherry
Cherry (sour)
Cherry compote
Cherry juice
Chestnut puree
Chestnuts
Chicken egg
Chicken egg white
Chicken meat
Chicken yolk
Chickpeas
Chili (pod or ground)
Chinese cabbage
Chives
Chlorella (fresh water)
Clarified butter
Clementine
Clementines
Cocoa
Coconut flakes
Coconut grated
Coconut meat
Coconut milk
Coffee
Cola drink
Cola drink (low calorie)
Corn germ oil
Cranberry
Cranberry jam
Crème fraiche cheese
Crispbread
Currant jam (black)
Currant jam (red)
Currant juice (black)
Currants (black)
Currants (red)
Dates dried
Dates red
Deer meat
Deer meat

Deer's Bones
Deer's kidneys
Ducks egg
Edam cheese
Evening primrose oil
Feta cheese
Fish innards
Fish remains
Fish sauce
French beans
Fresh cheese from soya
Fresh cheese with herbs
Fructose (glucose)
Fruit mix juice
Galangal
Garlic
Ginger oil
Goat
Goose egg
Gouda cheese
Grape juice red
Grape juice white
Grapes red
Grapes white
Grapeseed oil
Green spelt
Greengage
Halibut (Flatfish)
Hawthorn
Herring
Hijiki
Honey
Hop
Horse meat
Kaki plum
Kidney beans (red)
Kiwi
Kohlrabi
Lamb bones
Lamb meat
Lamb shoulder
Leek
Lemon
Lemon juice
Lemon peel
Lentils
Lentils black
Lentils red
Lentils yellow
Lima beans
Lime
Linseed oil
Mackerel
Mango juice

Mare's milk
Margarine
Margarine (diet)
Mirabelle plum
Miso paste (soy bean paste)
Morel (black, dried)
Morel, dried
Mu Erh Mushroom
Muesli
Mullet
Multi-grain bread (gray bread)
Mung bean
Mung bean sprouting
Mutton
Nectarine
Nori, purple seaweed, red algae
Olive oil
Onion (shallot)
Onion (spring onion)
Onion read
Onion white
Orange
Orange dried peel
Orange grated peel
Orange jam
Orange juice
Orange peel
Palm oil
Peaches
Peaches (canned)
Peanut oil
Peas
Peas, green
Pepper (ground)
Pepper Cayenne
Pepper powder (hot)
Pepper white (ground)
Peppercorns
Pepperoni
Pepperoni, red, pitted, halved
Pepperoni, yellow, pitted, halved
Peppers
Peppers (rose peppers)
Peppers (sweet)
Peppers powder
Pheasant
Pickle
Pigeon
Pigeon egg
Pineapple
Pineapplo (from a can)
Pineapple juice without sugar
Pinto beans speckled
Plaice

Plum
Plum dried
Plums
Poppy
Pork knuckle
Pork meat
Pumpkin seed oil
Quail
Quail egg
Rabbit
Rabbit (wild)
Rabbit meat
Radish
Radish (white, green, purple-red)
Radish black
Radish horseradish
Raisins
Raspberry jam
Red cabbage
Reishi mushroom
Rhubarb
Rice Basmati
Rice black
Rosefish
Rye
Rye flour
Sago (cereals)
Salmon
Salt
Salt (herbal)
Sauerkraut (cutted cabbage fermented)
Savory
Savoy cabbage / kale
Sea cucumber
Sesame oil
Sesame oil roasted
Shark
Shiitake, dried
Slug
Sour cherries
Sourdough
Soy sauce
Soya Cuisine (soy cream)
Soybean oil
Soybeans
Soybeans, black
Soybeans, blacks, fermented
Soybeans, yellow
Spurdog (spiny dogfish, Schillerlocken)
Strawberry jam
Strawberry Juice
Sugar - icing sugar
Sugar brown
Sugar candy white

Sugar cane sugar
Sugar molasses
Sugar palm sugar
Sugar substitute (sweetener)
Sugar white
Sunflower oil
Tabasco
Tangerine
Thistle oil
Tomato dried
Tuna
Turkey ham
Turnip
Umeboshi plums (Japanese apricots)
Vegetable juice

Vinegar (Apple vinegar)
Vinegar (Red wine vinegar)
Vinegar Aceto Balsamico
Vinegar Aceto Balsamico white
Walnut oil
Wheat
Wheat bulgur
Wheat germ oil
White beans
White cabbage
Whitefish
Wild boar meat
Wild garlic (garlic spinach)
Yeast

10.4 Do not use contra-acting foods

Adzuki beans
Almond
Almond marzipan
Almond milk
Almond puree
Anchovy / Sardine
Apricot
Apricot dried
Basic recipe for a duck soup
Beans (green, fresh)
Beef bone marrow
Beef heart
Beef heart (calf)
Beef kidney
Beef liver
Beef lungs (calf)
Beef stomach
Beer (alcohol-free)
Beer (alcohol-reduced)
Beer (Pils)
Beer (Top-fermented German dark beer)
Bitter liqueur
Brazil nuts
Brie cheese
Brown ale
Buttermilk
Camembert
Campari
Carp
Cashews
Chicken Blood
Chicken heart
Chicken liver
Chicken stomach
Chocolate

Chocolate (Diabetic)
Coconut fat
Coix (seeds) YiYi Ren
Cooking oil
Cottage cheese
Cow's milk (1.5% fat)
Cow's milk (whole milk 3.5% fat)
Cream (30% fat)
Cream sour 10%
Cream sour 20%
Cream sour 30%
Cream, sweet 30%
Creamer
Curd cheese 20%
Curd cheese 40%
Duck (heart)
Duck (slaughtered)
Eel
Eel smoked
Emmental cheese
Fernet Branca (herbal bitter liqueur)
Feta cheese
Fresh cheese
Gail plum
Ginseng liqueur
Goat and sheep's blood
Goat and sheep's brain
Goat and sheep's liver
Goat and sheep's milk
Goat and sheep's stomach
Goat cheese
Goose
Goose blood
Goose fat
Goose parts
Gorgonzola

Grass carp
Hazelnuts
Honey wine (Met)
Kefir
Lamb kidneys
Lamb liver
Linseed
Linseed (crushed)
Lychee liqueur
Manioc flour
Martini
Mayonnaise 50%
Mayonnaise 80%
Mineral water
Mold cheese
Mozzarella
Noodles (whole grain) with egg
Oat flakes (whole grain)
Oat meal
Olives
Olives green
Oyster mushroom
Parmesan
Peanut (roasted)
Peanut butter
Peanuts
Pig blood
Pine nuts
Pistachios
Pork Bacon
Pork brain
Pork fat (lard)
Pork heart
Pork kidneys
Pork Lard
Pork liver
Pork lung
Pork marrow bones
Pork sausage (Bratwurst)
Pork skin
Pork stomach
Pork/beef sausage (smoked)
Pork's intestine
Processed cheese 12%
processed cheese 30%
Prosecco

Psyllium seed
Puff pastry
Pumpernickel (dark bread)
Pumpkin seeds
Rabbit liver
Red wine
Rice (whole grain)
Rice red
Rice wild (nature rice)
Rum
Rye wholemeal bread
Sake
Sesame paste (Tahini)
Sesame, black
Sesame, white
Sheep's milk
Sheep's milk yoghurt
Sherry (whine)
Skim milk powder
Sour cream 15% fat
Sour milk
Sour milk cheese 20%
Spelled (Dark) bread
Spelled wholemeal flour
Spirit
Sugar fructose - fruit sugar
Sugar glucose - grapes sugar
Sugar Milk Sugar
Sunflower seeds
Toast bread (whole grain)
Walnuts
Walnuts roasted
Wheat beer
Wheat bran
Wheat flour whole grain
Wheat/Rye/Gray-black bread with yeast
Whey
White wine
Whole grain bread
Wholemeal flour
Wormwood
Yew nut
Yoghurt vanilla
Yogurt (natural, 1.5% fat)
Yogurt (natural, 3.5% fat)

11 Herbs and their effects

11.1 Basil

It has a beneficial effect on flatulence and nausea, relaxing and soothing. Good to fight emphysema, bronchitis, whooping cough, high blood pressure, headache, mouth odor, warts, hiccup, gout, migraine.

11.2 Mugwort

Reduces bleeding, alleviates pain. In the kitchen, mugwort is used as a spice for fat food. Since it contains many bitter substances, it boosts fat burning and promotes digestion.

11.3 Nettles

Promotes urination. Tea or juice, cleanses the blood and the kidneys, supports prostate problems, inhibit the formation of inflammation, pain-relieving.

11.4 Catuaba tea

High proportion of minerals and trace elements. Magnesium, potassium and calcium in particular are obtained in considerable quantities. Catuaba is refreshing.

11.5 Chamomile

Antispasmodic and anti-inflammatory for digestive disorders, soothes the nerves and promotes good sleep. Applied externally, it heals wounds in the mouth-throat area and the skin. Strengthens eyesight.

11.6 Coriander

The essential oils are appetizing, digestive, cramping and soothing in stomach and intestinal disorders.

11.7 Herbs various

Appetizing, lots of trace elements and vitamins

11.8 Cress

Diuretic, supports urination. Good to fight dry mouth, inner agitation, sore throat, diabetes, kidney stones, gastrointestinal complaints, lung problems, menstrual cramps or cancer.

11.9 Chives

Bactericide, prevents cancer, strengthens gastric juice production, promotes digestion and blood circulation, promotes growth, triggers stagnation.

11.10   Lovage

Stimulates digestion, reduces pain. Extracts of the root are used to flush out urinary tract infections and prevent kidney gravel.

11.11   Dandelion (young plants)

Detoxifies, relieves inflammation. Regulates digestion, helps with rheumatism, releases kidney stones, leaves pimples and chronic skin disorders disappear.

11.12   Oregano dried

It has an anti-digestive, calming and nerve-strengthening effect, helps to fight cramping stomach and intestinal disorders. The ingredient Carvacrol has an anti-inflammatory effect.

11.13   Parsley

Stimulates liver function, detoxifies. Forces urinating. Relieves flatulence. Digestive and menstrual stimulating, birth-accelerating, memory-enhancing, blood-purifying, skin-smoothing.

11.14   Peppermint

Relaxes, frees the lungs and the nose (inhale), regulates the cycle. Stimulates bile flow and bile production, antispasmodic in gastrointestinal disorders, antimicrobial and antiviral.

11.15   Rosemary

Promotes digestion, relieves bloating, strengthens lung, spleen and kidney. Affects the circulation and nerves.
Appetizing. Baths help to fight circulatory disorders as well as with gout and rheumatism.

11.16 Sage

Good to fight yeast infections. The leaves have a digestive effect and are used in greasy foods. Antiperspirant effect. Helps to relieve coughing attacks. Dries out (TCM).

11.17 Thyme dried

Disinfecting. It stimulates the blood circulation, increases the appetite and helps to digest fat meat better. Strengthens lungs and spleen (TCM).

11.18 Lemon Balm (fresh)

Stimulating, antibacterial, encouraging, relaxing, antispasmodic, cooling, antipyretic, analgesic, sweat-inducing, virus-inhibiting. Good for colds, fever, flu, cough, bronchitis, asthma, loss of appetite, bloating, heartburn.

12 Basics of Nutrition

The basic principles of nutrition described herein are general recommendations. They are not aimed at a specific form of therapy. Recommendations concerning a therapy have priority.

12.1 Nutrition

Regular meals in a relaxed atmosphere. A warm breakfast is considered a good start into the day.
The main meals ought to be taken for lunch – supper in the early evening. Pay attention to feeling hungry or sated: don't eat too much nor remain hungry is the rule
Prepare the meals freshly from natural, regional products. Frozen, heat-conserved, industrially prepared or foodstuffs cooked in the microwave oven are rejected.
Choice of foodstuffs according to the season: more cooling food in summer, more warming food in winter.
Eat cooked food at least twice a day. Food and drinks ought to be lukewarm, never ice-cold or hot.
Raw vegetables, briefly cooked vegetables, freshly squeezed juices and mineral water are not recommended. Milk and dairy products are only included in the diet if they don't cause problems.
Don't use therapeutic recipes over a longer period without consulting your doctor or therapist.

Varied food
Enjoy the diversity of foodstuffs. Characteristics of a balanced nutrition are variety, suitable combination and a balanced quantity of rich and low energy foodstuffs (on one hand avoiding undersupply with essential nutrients and on the other hand to take to many undesirable substances).

A lot of Cereal Products - and Potatoes
Bread, pasta, rice, cereal flakes (best wholemeal) as well as potatoes contain almost no fat, but many vitamins, mineral nutrients, trace elements, roughage and secondary plant substances. These foodstuffs ought to be taken with low-fat side dishes.

Vegetables and Fruit – „Take Five" every day …
5 portions of vegetables and fruit a day, as fresh as possible, briefly cooked, or maybe one portion as a juice – ideal as a side dish to every meal as well as snack between meals: Thus a lot of vitamins, mineral nutrients as well as roughage and secondary plant substances

Daily milk and dairy products

Milk and Dairy Products every Day, once or twice per Week Fish; meat, sausages as well as eggs moderately. These foodstuffs contain valuable nutrients like calcium in the milk, iodine selenium and omega-3 fat acids in saltwater fish. Meat is favorable due to its high content of disposable iron and the vitamins B1, B6 and B12. Quantities of 300 – 600 g meat and sausage per week are sufficient. Prefer low-fat products, especially in meat- and dairy products.

Low-fat and fatty Foodstuffs

Fat supplies us with essential fat acids and fatty foodstuffs contain also fat-soluble vitamins. Fat is high in energy; therefore much fat in the food may cause overweight, possibly also cancer. Too many saturated fat acids may further a tendency for cardio-vascular diseases in the long term. Prefer vegetable oils and fats (e.g. rapeseed-, olive-, soya-oils and solid fats produced therefrom). Beware of invisible fat in meat- and dairy products, pastry and sweets as well as in fast-food and convenience foods. 70 – 90 g fat per day is sufficient.

Moderately Sugar and Salt

Take sugar and foods/drinks containing various kinds of sugar (e.g. glucose syrup) only occasionally. Use herbs and spices as well as a little salt creatively. Prefer salt containing iodine.

Plenty of Liquids

Water is absolutely essential. Drink 1-2 l liquids every day. Prefer water (with or without gas) and other low-calorie drinks. Alcoholic drinks should not be taken.

Tasty Dishes, carefully cooked

Cook the meals with as low temperatures and as short as possible, using little water and fat – this preserves the original taste, keeps the nutrients intact and prevents the production of harmful compounds.

Take time and enjoy the food

Take your Time and enjoy your Food
Eating consciously helps to eat right. The eye enjoys food, too. It's fun, invites to enjoy varied dishes and stimulates the feeling of satiety.

Watch your Weight and stay in Motion

A balanced diet and a lot of exercise and sport (30 – 60 min/day) are a healthy combination. The right weight furthers well-being and health. Thermals, directional effectiveness, digestive power

There are various criteria for judging the effectiveness of herbs and foodstuffs.

The use of certain herbs and ingredients is based on observations of the effects on the body which these foodstuffs, herbs and spices show after having eaten them. The medical science has developed following system: Every ingredient or herb has a directional effectiveness. Furthermore, there are herbs which have a special effect on certain organs.

The basic condition for a healthy metabolism is to obtain sufficient energy from food and that the digestive process doesn't use too much energy. An easily digestible meal makes content and sated, doesn't cause flatulence and fatigue after the meal. The perfect spices increase the healthiness of our meals. Very often, just small doses of herbs and spices will suffice. They are not used to make us sated, but to help our digestive organs to digest the food.

12.2 Recipes

The recipes list the ingredients to be used and the cooking instructions show how the dish is prepared. The list of ingredients shows the concerned quantities as well as the relevance for the therapy. If you find „less than mentioned", try to comply or find an alternative from the „list of recommended foodstuffs". Mostly it shall result just in a small change of taste when you simply avoid this ingredient.

Mild cooking methods: boiling, stewing, poaching, steaming
Strong cooking methods: barbecuing, roasting, frying, smoking
Balanced cooking methods: deep-frying, baking brick
Deep-freezing and warming in the microwave oven should be avoided (denaturalization).

12.3 Foodstuffs

Foodstuffs have an effect on body and soul like medicinal herbs, only a very much milder one. Dietary advice is mainly based on regional foodstuffs. The knowledge about the effects of each foodstuff and the knowledge, when which foodstuff shall be used, is based on the orthodox school of medicine. Use ecologic-organic products, if possible. As everything should be cooked for a long time due to a better digestability and very rarely eaten raw, the food agrees with everyone.

The classification of the foodstuffs according to their effect on the body is the basis in order to achieve a harmonious status of health

Dietary advisors do not recommend certain foodstuffs for everyone. The individual diet is tailor-made for the individual constitution.

Buy only fresh and ripe fruit and vegetables. You ought to leave unripe fruit and vegetables and such with brown spots and wilted leaves behind in the market. In this case take deep-frozen goods (never ready-to-serve dishes!). Fruit and vegetables are deep-frozen immediately after harvesting and often contain more vitamins and minerals than the goods from the vegetable shelf. Whereas conserved or tinned goods contain very much less biological substances. Also, salt, sugar and others are mostly added to the latter. Never leave the foodstuffs in the water after washing them to avoid that many vital substances get drowned. Clean salads, fruit and vegetables immediately before serving.

Please make sure of the hygienic processing of foodstuffs. Clean your salads, fruit and vegetables carefully. When cooking with meat, prepare all ingredients first and then process the meat products. Clean the worktop and tools very carefully. Wooden surfaces ought to be treated with a mild disinfectant regularly in order to reduce germination.

Store fruit and vegetables separately, if possible. Harvested fruit and vegetables are still alive and emit e.g. ethylene gas, which makes other products ripen and age faster. Keep meat and fish in the closed packaging or store them in the fridge in closed containers.

12.4 Herbs

There are some basic rules for storing medicinal herbs. On principle, herbs must be protected from direct sunlight, humidity and heat.

Containers for the storage of herbs may be glasses, ceramic jars and even plastic containers. However, plastic is a rather unsuitable material and should only be a short-term solution. In case of glass containers, use a dark material.

Medicinal herbs cannot be kept for any long period. The shelf life of herbs is limited. However, it can be prolonged with suitable storage. The place should be dark, rather cool and absolutely dry. A wooden medicine cabinet, placed not directly next to a source of heat, would be ideal. Never buy large quantities of herbs so as not to have to throw them away. Label the container with the name of the herb and the date of harvesting or processing.

13 Other dietic-books

The following syndromes of dietetics, TCM or for a therapy supplement for cancer are available.

Dietetics

E001. Nutrition of the infant - baby food
E002. Nutrition during lactation
E003. Nutrition in old age
E004. Nutrition of children and adolescents
E005. Nutrition of athletes
E006. Light weight
E007. Pregnancy
E008. Full food

Protein and electrolyte - kidneys
E009. (hemodialysis) dialysis treatment
E010. Acute renal failure
E011. Chronic renal insufficiency
E012. Nephrotic syndrome
E013. Kidney stones (nephrolithiasis)

Gastrointestinal tract - pancreas
E014. Acute pancreatitis (inflammation of the pancreas)
E015. Chronic pancreatitis (inflammation of the pancreas)

Gastrointestinal tract - small intestine and large intestine
E016. Acute obstipation (constipation)
E017. Chronic obstipation (constipation)
E018. Colon irritabile
E019. Diverticulitis
E020. Acquired lactose intolerance (lactose malabsorption)
E021. Fructose malabsorption
E022. Glutensensitive enteropathy (celiac disease)
E023. Colectomy
E024. Short Bowel Syndrome

Gastrointestinal tract - liver, gallbladder, bile ducts
E025. Acute and chronic hepatitis (inflammation of the liver)
E026. Cholelithiasis (bile stones)
E027. fatty liver
E028. cirrhosis

Gastrointestinal tract - Stomach and duodenal intestine
E029. Acute gastritis
E030. Chronic gastritis
E031. Stomach bleeding
E032. Ulcus ventriculi and duodenal ulcer
E033. Condition after gastric surgery

Gastrointestinal tract - oral cavity and esophagus
E034. Stomatitis
E035. Esophageal carcinoma (esophageal cancer)
E036. Refluosophagitis (heartburn)

Special diseases
E037. Phenylketonuria (PKU)
E038. Rheumatic joint diseases

Metabolism
E039. Obesity (overweight)
E040. Diabetes mellitus
E041. Eating disorders (underweight)

Fat metabolism
E042. Hypercholesterolaemia (increased cholesterol level)
E043. Hepatic Encephalopathy

Heart and circulation
E044. Arteriosclerosis (arterial calcification)
E045. Heart insufficiency
E046. Hypertension
E047. Hyperuricaemia and gout

Changed nutrient requirements
E048. In case of fever
E049. For malignant diseases
E050. After burns
E051. Radiation and chemotherapy

CANCER
E100. Pancreatic cancer
E101. Bladder cancer
E102. Blood cancer (leukemia)
E103. Breast cancer
E104. Colorectal cancer
E105. Gastric cancer
E106. Kidney cancer
E107. Esophageal cancer

TCM
E200. Bladder - moisture heat in the bladder
E201. Bladder - moisture and cold in the bladder
E202. Bladder - emptiness and cold in the bladder
E203. Large intestine - external cold affects the large intestine
E204. Large intestine - moisture heat in the large intestine
E205. Large intestine - heat blocks the intestine II acute
E206. Large intestine - dryness of the colon
E207. Large intestine - Yang deficiency (cold)
E208. Heart - Blood insufficiency
E209. Heart - Blood stagnation
E210. Heart - Fire
E211. Heart - Hot mucus clogs the heart pores

E212. Heart - Cold mucus clogs the heart pores
E213. Heart - Qi deficiency
E214. Heart - Yang deficiency
E215. Heart - Yin deficiency
E216. Liver - Ascending Liver Yang
E217. Liver - Blood deficiency
E218. Liver - Blood stagnation
E219. Liver - Moisture heat in liver and gall bladder
E220. Liver - Fire
E221. Liver - Gall bladder Qi-Empty
E222. Liver - Cold in the liver meridian
E223. Liver - Qi stagnation
E224. Liver - Wind
E225. Liver - Wind with ascending liver Yang
E226. Liver - Wind with blood anemic
E227. Liver - Wind with extreme heat
E228. Lung - Qi deficiency
E229. Lung - Mucus-moisture in the lungs
E230. Lung - Mucus-heat in the lungs
E231. Lung - Mucus-cold in the lungs
E232. Lung - Dryness of the lungs
E233. Lung - Wind-heat attacks the lungs
E234. Lung - Wind-cold affects the lungs
E235. Lung - Yin deficiency
E236. Stomach - Bloodstagnation
E237. Stomach - Fire
E238. Stomach - Cold with liquid
E239. Stomach - Nutrition stagnation
E240. Stomach - Qi deficiency
E241. Stomach - Rebellious Qi
E242. Stomach - Yin Emptiness
E243. Spleen - Heat and moisture attack the spleen
E244. Spleen - Coldness and moisture affects the spleen
E245. Spleen - Qi deficiency
E246. Spleen - Qi deficiency + Declining spleen Qi
E247. Spleen - Qi deficiency + spleen does not control the blood
E248. Spleen - Yang deficiency
E249. Kidney - Heart and kidney no longer communicate
E250. Kidney - Jing deficiency
E251. Kidney - Kidneys cannot receive the Qi
E252. Kidney - Qi is not stable
E253. Kidney - Yang deficiency
E254. Kidney - Yin deficiency

For further information visit di-book.com.